YOUR CHILD'S FIRST CONFESSION

Introduction

THE SACRAMENT OF RECONCILIATION IS seen in many different lights. For some, it is a way of renewing and refreshing their relationship with God. For others, it is more an experience of embarrassment mixed with fear and self-consciousness. Inevitably, too, it is a favourite subject for jokes both inside and outside the Church.

As you prepare your child for the Sacrament of the Reconciliation, it's important to look at the different images of Confession and also to look at the truth about the Sacrament.

You and your partner will have your own personal impressions and experiences of Confession and these provide a valuable starting point for the preparation of your child for the Sacrament of Reconciliation.

As a loving and caring parent you will be anxious to help your child at this important time, and of course, you are at the very heart of your child's understanding of Reconciliation. We hope that this book will help you clarify your own approach to the Sacrament and so enable you to provide creative support for your child during the preparation period.

contents

How do you feel about Confession?	2
Memories of Confession	3
What is Reconciliation?	4
God and his People	5
How did Jesus Christ receive sinners?	6
The history of the Sacrament of Reconciliation	8
What happens at Confession?	10
Reconciliation – then and now	12
Questions and Answers	14
Parents are the key to love	16

HOW DO YOU FEEL ABOUT CONFESSION?

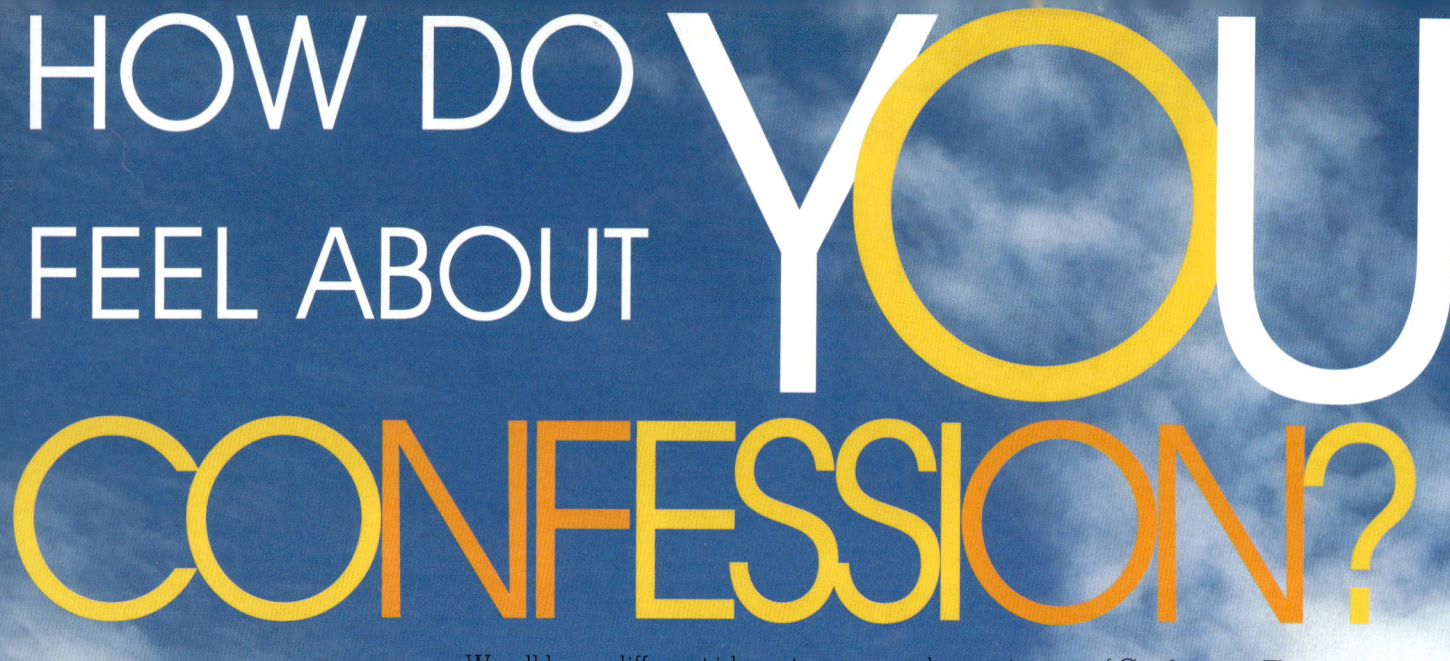

We all have different ideas, images and experiences of Confession. These may be based upon what we have seen or heard, what we have read – either as truth or fiction or they may be pictures conjured up in our own minds about what really goes on in Confession – especially other peoples' confessions!

If you are a Catholic you will have your own memories of your First Confession. You will have had good experiences and probably some bad experiences of Confession too. You may go regularly to Confession or you may have given up going – either for a specific reason or simply because you've got out of the habit.

If you're not a Catholic, your picture of Confession will inevitably be second-hand. You will probably have seen people going to Confession either in a Catholic Church, in films or on TV. You may find it a rather difficult activity to understand. There can be something unnerving, frightening or embarrassing about the idea of telling someone, perhaps a stranger, about all the bad things you've done. It's especially difficult to understand if that all takes place in a little dark room in whispered voices. In fact, you may feel deeply concerned about what you are about to subject your child to in the name of being a Christian.

Before you prepare for your child's First Confession then, it's important to clarify a number of points for yourself and for your partner.

Take some time to think about the following questions and then share your ideas on the subject:

- How do you feel about Confession?
- Have you been to Confession yourself? If so, how was it for you? If not, what do you think it would be like for you?
- What is your best image/experience of Confession?
- What is your worst image/experience of Confession?
- How often do you go to Confession yourself – Regularly... Annually... Never...?
- If you go regularly or annually, can you say why?
- If you never go to Confession yourself, can you say why?

We can have a very precious memory of Confession which has given us a touchstone on which to base our whole relationship with God and with our faith.

We can have a very painful memory of Confession which has clouded our vision and our understanding of the value of this sacrament and of the nature of God.

MEMORIES OF CONFESSION

For many years we have centred this sacrament on confession; the confession of our sins. This can give a false picture because the focus in this sacrament is not what we do or say. In fact this sacrament has very little to do with the listing of sins but everything to do with being reconciled to God and to our Christian community when we have moved away from both.

Memories are powerful. They linger in our hearts and minds long after the event but they rarely tell the whole story, rarely offer the full picture. Why not use this opportunity of your child's First Confession to renew and refresh and develop your own understanding of the true nature of this sacrament as Jesus Christ initiated it?

WHAT IS RECONCILIATION?

To understand our humanity, what it is to be human, we need to look at Jesus Christ. Jesus was truly God; he was the Son who lived amongst us as a fully human person. He was exactly the same as us in all things. He ate like us, he laughed and cried like us, he loved like us and he suffered like us. The only difference between Jesus' humanity and ours was that sin played no part in his life. He did not sin. And the reason he did not sin was because he was truly human. He was fully human exactly as God had intended every man and woman to be. He is a pattern for humanity. Jesus shows us what it is to be a true and complete human being.

Sin

Sin enters our life when we are less than human. Every time we think, say or do something which is not a reflection of Jesus' humanity, we are less than human; we sin. But sin doesn't stop there because so much of what we do or fail to do affects other people. The knock-on effect of damaging relationships, isolation, breakdowns in communication, all serve to cut us off from others and so distort and damage people. We even say in extreme cases, "He/she's like an animal!" What we're saying when we say that is in a sense true – that person is less than fully human, but then so are those who caused that distortion or damage; that isolation. It's easy to see that sin damages not only individuals but also whole communities.

Becoming fully human

Even in the first accounts of the early Church we can read about tensions, disagreements and rejection within this community of believers. Clearly, in spite of all that they had experienced, they remained fragile and many of them carried within them the damage caused by sin (by being less than human) from past years.

No one becomes fully human overnight or even in a year or two. It takes time. And while we are growing towards full humanity we need help. As we have seen, during his life on earth, Jesus recognised this and constantly offered healing and reconciliation to the people he met.

Divisive

Throughout his life Jesus worked and preached endlessly amongst all sorts of people to bring down the barriers which divided them. He emphasised over and over again that we are all God's children, we are his family, his Chosen People. Following his resurrection, Jesus' followers gathered together and became a community. They were united in that they were listening to the words of Jesus and experiencing his active love in the work of his Spirit in their lives. They knew what it was to be fully human but they were also still very weak and easily discouraged.

Peace & Reconciliation

Following his resurrection, he appeared to his disciples, his followers, and offered them first of all his Peace. As they were gathered together, full of shame about the way they had deserted him, full of fear about their future and full of questions about who he really was, Christ came to them. And his first word was "Peace". The overwhelming love of God washed over them all. Everything else could wait, the words of regret, sorrow and shame. The most important point Jesus wanted to make was that he loved them, he understood them and he wanted to restore any damage to their relationship with him. Jesus then continued:
"As the Father sent me,
so I am sending you."
After saying this he breathed on them and said:
"Receive the Holy Spirit.
For those whose sins you forgive,
they are forgiven; for those whose sins you retain,
they are retained."

He asks his followers to continue his work. To enable them to do this he promises the gift of his Holy Spirit. The Holy Spirit will be with them to guide them, heal them and to infuse them with Christ's Spirit of reconciliation.

Parents and Reconciliation

God's forgiving, healing love is not to be kept as a personal "keep clean" kit, but it is to grow, spread and develop amongst all his followers. In loving, forgiving and healing one another, we build the body of Christ, the Church, in the world in every time and in every place. Christians make Christ present in their lives by their words and actions of love and reconciliation and peacemaking.

As a Christian parent, you are laying the foundation for your child's life. You are called to place at the heart of your parenting, Christ's Spirit of unconditional love, forgiveness and reconciliation. As your child experiences this in your care, he or she will begin to glimpse the true nature of the love of God and the promise of lasting peace and happiness, which is God's promise to us.

> "I have formed you... I will not forget you.
> I have dispelled your faults like a cloud,
> your sins like a mist.
> Come back to me,
> for I have redeemed you."
> **Isaiah 44:21-22**

GOD AND HIS PEOPLE

The Bible, the Old Testament and the New Testament, carries the history of God's relationship with men and women. This history is told in story, parable, historical fact, poetry and in prophecy, but one thing is abundantly clear from start to finish; God constantly seeks reconciliation with men and women.

In the beginning

The very beginning of this story of our relationship with God begins with a break in the unity which man and women shared with their Creator. This break with God is immediately followed by division, discord and murder between men themselves in the story of Cain and Abel.

From then onwards a continuing story unfolds of God reaching out in love and forgiveness to his people. Even in the Old Testament with its often blood-thirsty stories of revenge, killing and jealousies, God is a God of pardon and forgiveness.

> "Come now, let us talk this over, says the Lord.
> Though your sins are like scarlet, they shall be as white as snow.
> Though they are red as crimson, they shall be like wool."
> **Isaiah 1:18.**

Yet over and over again we read of men and women unable or unwilling to accept his gift of forgiveness and reconciliation. So often they resist true reconciliation with the heavenly Father. From time to time they turn back to him in fear, desperation, in moments of religious fervour, only to fall away again in the face of temptation, challenge or pressure from unbelievers.

The patience of God

Unable to recognise or comprehend the full reality of a God who is totally committed to them, totally healing, totally loving and understanding, men and women failed to grasp what an intimate, loving relationship with God really meant, despite what their history and experience taught them. But unlike men and women, God doesn't seek revenge all he asks for is that his people turn back to him.

The Old Testament is a record of a People's growing experience and understanding of God and themselves. It's an important part of men and women's experience because it shows us over and over again the ways in which God reveal himself in the ordinary experiences of life. But the Old Testament was incomplete because the God of the Old Testament inevitably remained, in a certain sense, remote.

Jesus is the Pattern

The coming of Jesus Christ brought men and women's experience of God into everyday life. Jesus Christ told us and showed us what it is to be united with his Father. Jesus Christ re-established for all of us that unity and intimate friendship with God which was rejected in the beginning by man and woman.

HOW DID JESUS RECEIVE SINNERS?

The woman caught in adultery

The scribes and the Pharisees brought a woman along who had been caught committing adultery; and making her stand in full view of everybody, they said to Jesus, 'Master, this woman was caught in the very act of committing adultery, and Moses has ordered us in the Law to condemn women like this to death by stoning. What have you to say?' They asked him this as a test, looking for something to use against him. But Jesus bent down and started writing on the ground with his finger. As they persisted with their question, he looked up and said, 'If there is one of you who has not sinned let him be the first to throw a stone at her.' Then he bent down and wrote on the ground again. When they heard this they went away one by one, beginning with the eldest, until Jesus was left alone with the woman who remained standing there. He looked up and said, 'Woman where are they? has no one condemned you?' 'No one sir,' she replied. 'Neither do I condemn you,' said Jesus 'go away, and don't sin any more.'
John 8: 3-11.

As her self-righteous accusers walk away, the woman stands in silence before Christ. She makes no confession, offers no excuses, she stands exposed and vulnerable. Her sinfulness, her failure, clear for all to see.

Jesus, reflecting the love of an all-knowing, all-seeing Father, reassures her that he does not condemn her. He simply says, "Don't sin any more". In other words, he invites her to a conversion to a new way of living. Jesus says effectively, "Don't turn away from your heavenly Father any more. Come, be united with your loving God who heals you, forgives you, cares for you."

The wayward and selfish son

A man had two sons. The younger said to his father, 'Father, let me have my share of the estate that would come to me'. So the father divided the property between them. A few days later the younger son got together everything he had and left for a distant country where he squandered everything he had on a life of debauchery. When he had spent it all, that country experienced a severe famine, and now he began to feel the pinch, so he hired himself out to one of the local inhabitants who put him on his farm to feed the pigs. And he would willingly have filled his belly with the husks the pigs were eating but no one offered him anything. Then he came to his senses and said, 'How many of my father's paid servants have more food than they want, and here am I dying of hunger! I will leave this place and go to my father and say: Father, I have sinned against heaven and against you; I no longer deserve to be called your son; treat me as one of your paid servants.'
So he left the place and went back to his father.

While he was still a long way off, his father saw him and was moved with pity. He ran to the boy, clasped him in his arms and kissed him tenderly. Then his son said, 'Father, I have sinned against heaven and against you. I no longer deserve to be called your son.' But the father said to his servants, 'Quick! Bring out the best robe and put it on him; put a ring on his finger and sandals on his feet. Bring the calf we have been fattening, and kill it; we are going to have a feast, a celebration, because this son of mine was dead and has come back to life; he was lost and is found.' And they all began to celebrate.
Luke 15: 11-24.

Jesus tells this story to illustrate clearly the nature of his Father's forgiveness and his compassionate love for us. The younger son has squandered every gift his father ever gave him. He has wasted even his life and now he "feels the pinch", he trails home to Dad. Even the most casual onlooker can see that this lad is not overcome with grief and sorrow at his failures and wastefulness. He simply recognises that there's no future in the way he is going.

The welcome he gets exceeds all expectations anyone could have had. His father, who is looking out for him, runs to meet him halfway, holds him close, restores him to complete unity as his beloved child in his home. That is the way God welcomes us the minute we make the first move.

Jesus meets a notorious sinner

One of the Pharisees invited him to a meal. When he arrived at the Pharisee's house and took his place at table, a woman came in, who had a bad name in the town. She had heard he was dining with the Pharisee and had brought with her an alabaster jar of ointment. She waited behind him at his feet, weeping, and her tears fell on his feet, and she wiped them away with her hair; then she covered his feet with kisses and anointed them with ointment.

When the Pharisee who had invited him saw this, he said to himself, 'If this man were a prophet, he would know who this woman is that is touching him and what a bad name she has'. Then Jesus took him up and said,'Simon, I have something to say to you'. 'Speak, Master' was the reply. 'There was once a creditor who had two men in his debt; one owed him five hundred denarii, the other fifty. They were unable to pay, so he pardoned them both. Which of them will love him more?' 'The one who was pardoned more, I suppose' answered Simon. Jesus said, 'You are right'.

Then he turned to the woman, 'Simon,' he said 'you see this woman? I came into your house, and you poured no water over my feet, but she has poured out her tears over my feet and wiped them with her hair. You gave me no kiss, but she has been covering my feet with kisses ever since I came in.

You did not anoint my head with oil, but she has anointed my feet with ointment. For this reason I tell you that her sins, her many sins, must have been forgiven her, or she would not have shown such great love.' Then he said to her, 'Your sins are forgiven'. Those who were with him at table began to say to themselves,' Who is this man, that he even forgives sins?'

But he said to the woman, 'Your faith has saved you; go in peace.'
Luke 7:36-50.

This is a very human story. Everyone present knows what kind of a woman this is. Everyone knows she is bad news, a hopeless case, and not the sort of person to be seen with if you value your reputation. She knows it too, and is overcome with sadness, despair and grief. She has no pride left, only a desperate longing to make peace, to get in touch once again with goodness, with wholeness. Self-righteousness blinds the others present, but Jesus knows the desire in her heart for reconciliation; he sees her tears of repentance and her faith in his healing love. Again, there are no recriminations, no picking over her failures, her sinfulness. Forgiveness and reconciliation are hers even before the words are said because of the faith she displays in Christ's ability to heal her. As Jesus says, "Her sins, her many sins, must have been forgiven her, or she would not have shown such great love."

The paralytic man

Some people appeared, bringing him a paralytic stretched out on a bed. Seeing their faith, Jesus said to the paralytic, 'Courage, my child, your sins are forgiven'. And at this some scribes said to themselves, 'This man is blaspheming'. Knowing what was in their minds Jesus said, 'Why do you have such wicked thoughts in your hearts? Now which of these is easier: to say. 'Your sins are forgiven', or to say, 'Get up and walk'? But to prove to you that the Son of Man has authority on earth to forgive sins' - he said to the paralytic – 'get up, and pick up your bed and go off home'.
And the man got up and went home.
Matthew 9: 2-7.

This man is so disabled that he cannot do anything for himself. His friends carry him to Jesus. Once again, we see onlookers who are set on criticism and judging others. When we recall that, traditionally, sickness was seen as God's punishment for sin committed either by the sufferer or his or her parents, this healing is especially significant. Jesus' words, "Your sins are forgiven you" floor the onlookers because Jesus is concerned with wholeness of mind and body. He proves that he is the Son of God by showing his power to forgive sin in a way that the onlookers will understand – by healing the man. Again, it is the faith that the sinner and his friends have in Jesus, which brings them to seek the forgiveness and reconciliation which unites them to Christ.

The ancient Greek and Hebrew words for forgiveness mean 'to let go', 'to set free', 'to cover', 'to pardon'; in fact to re-establish what was intact before. And throughout the gospels we see Jesus revealing in a real and very human way a God of forgiveness and pardon. Far from seeking revenge, all God asks is that his people turn back to him. And in turning to the Lord, in accepting his gift of forgiveness and reconciliation, true healing of mind, soul and body takes place.

It's interesting that Christ imposes no punishment or condemnation. He offers simple, unconditional love for the sinner. There is acceptance of the value and worth of the individual regardless of their sin. There is belief too, in the sincerity of the sinner, however poor their track record may be. Every act of God's forgiveness is indeed a new beginning. Once such a relationship, such a love is accepted, (and that can be difficult, as we see from the reactions of the scribes and Pharisees), true freedom is found.

It is a freedom from slavery to sin and a solution to meeting our needs and weaknesses. It is a freedom to live as a warmly accepted friend of Jesus Christ, a freedom to live in trust and hope as a result of our confidence in the gift of God's unconditional love.

THE HISTORY OF THE SACRAMENT OF RECONCILIATION

Jesus

Jesus teaches his disciples about forgiveness and reconciliation through his encounters with people during his lifetime, in his parables and in his words to them following the resurrection:

"As the Father sent me,
so I am sending you."
After saying this he breathed on them
and said:
"Receive the Holy Spirit.
For those whose sins you forgive,
they are forgiven;
for those whose sins you retain,
they are retained."
John 20: 21-23.

The First Christians

Guided by the teaching of Christ and through his Holy Spirit, the first Christians practised forgiveness and reconciliation amongst themselves, guiding, strengthening and advising one another as brothers and sisters of Christ through their common baptism. St Paul writes:
"Since the Spirit is our life, let us be directed by the Spirit. We must stop being conceited, provocative and envious.
If one of you misbehaves, the more spiritual of you who set him right should do so in a spirit of gentleness, not forgetting that you may be tempted yourselves. You should carry each other's troubles and fulfil the law of Christ."
Galatians 5:26. 6:1-2.

The Early Church

Whilst the followers of Christ supported one another in spiritual guidance and reconciliation in their day to day lives, the early Church used Baptism and to a lesser extent, Anointing of the Sick, as the main channels of forgiveness. Converts at that time accepted the faith knowing full well that it might mean death. To fall away from such a deliberate commitment to Christ was unthinkable. But some did subsequently deny their faith in Jesus Christ (apostasy) or commit a serious sin which brought scandal upon the Christian community.

Afterwards many were sorry and wished to be re-admitted to the Church. They could not be re-baptised so a public Ceremony of Forgiveness became the practice. It usually involved the following:

1. Public confession of sin to the Bishop.
2. There were only three official, or recognised sins against the community: murder, apostasy and adultery.
3. Only one confession was allowed in a lifetime (none for priests).
4. Long and severe public penance (fasting, sackcloth and ashes).
5. Only after all the above was absolution received from the Bishop by the laying on of hands.

The Fourth Century

In the fourth century St Augustine urged young people not to receive the sacrament because it made ordinary life afterwards impossible: they could not get married, become a priest or join the army or professions. Very many people put it off until their deathbed for this reason and also because the whole thing was so harsh. It became very clear who was a sinner and who was penitent. Penance became not healing and reconciling but punishing and loaded with penalties. As a result, the sacrament almost died out. Well intentioned zeal had eclipsed the Spirit of the Christ of the Gospels.

The Middle Ages

Christians however, still felt the need to draw closer to God and to renew and reconcile their lives to Christ. By the Middle Ages Irish missionary monks and nuns began to see Christians individually and in private to offer spiritual guidance.
They helped them with their examination of conscience and in making their peace with God in the privacy of a one to one encounter. These monks and nuns offered guidance and suggested ways in which a sinner could do penance and "make up" to God for their sins. This form of confession became very popular although it was at first condemned by the bishops as a permissive novelty. Finally, the popularity overcame ecclesiastical reservations and it was officially accepted. There were three main differences to earlier practice:
1. Private confession of sin to a priest (not just bishops as before).
2. Confessions became more frequent and included a wider range of less serious sin.
3. A penance was given to be performed after absolution was given.
Penance was now respectable but a sort of tarriff of penances for different sins became usual.
For example:
For murder – three years exile on bread and water plus three more years as a servant to the victim's family.
For drunkenness – three weeks bread and water.
For horse stealing – three Lents.
After the Battle of Hastings, the Norman soldiers got one year's penance for each man they killed and forty days for those they wounded. The archers got three Lents each!

The late Middle Ages

In the late Middle Ages the sacraments were more strictly defined in name and number. Penance now had three essential elements: contrition (sorrow), confession and satisfaction. Of course, we cannot "satisfy" God for sin but our penance is a token of our desire to make up. The custom began of giving prayers instead of physical penance, then offering a stipend for a priest to say Mass (the most perfect prayer). Then giving money instead (Battle Abbey was built on the proceeds of the almsgiving of soldiers). And then the rich began paying others to do their penances! For instance, a man with a penance of seven years bread and water could pay twelve men to fast three days and one hundred and twenty men to do three days seven times:
$12 \times 3 + 120 \times 7 \times 3 = 2,556$ days = 7 years!
This sort of abuse and the related question of Indulgences was one of the causes of the Reformation.

Great emphasis was now placed on the seal of secrecy on the part of the confessor. In the sixteenth century, St Charles Borromeo apparently invented the confessional box. The Council of Trent established the practice of Confession as we have known it for the last four hundred years.

Second Vatican Council

The Second Vatican Council in the early 1960's took a fresh look at the way we celebrate the sacraments so that we could learn from the mistakes of history and from our growing understanding of human psychology, behavioural sciences and research and the growth of knowledge about the life of Christ and his earliest followers. The Church, both the people and the institution, had moved a long way from the way Christ received sinners in the gospel.

Vatican II renewed the Church in many fundamental ways often reconciling modern practice of the Christian life with that of the New Testament and the first Christians. It did not simply suggest therefore yet another new way of going to Confession but urged us to think about our attitudes to sin, forgiveness, guilt, reconciliation and repentance. We are called continually to repent and repent does not just mean being sorry, it means change.

Confession had become a very private affair. Each person became responsible for keeping themselves as squeaky-clean and sin-free as possible in order to gain merit in the eyes of God and to be assured of eternal life. The community aspect of sin was lost whilst there was a danger of too much introspection by individuals which can lead to scrupulosity and lack of confidence in the action of the Holy Spirit in the life of a Christian.

Today, the Church is rediscovering the full richness and love offered by Christ to his followers in this healing and encouraging sacrament in her restoration of the emphasis on reconciliation rather than simply confessing sins.

WHAT HAPPENS AT CONFE

People who are not Catholics often wonder what happens at Confession and even Catholics can lose sight of the true nature of this sacrament. Now that you are helping your child prepare for their first celebration of the Sacrament of Reconciliation, it's good to refresh our memories or get to know exactly what your child will be celebrating.

There's a saying that "a leopard cannot change its spots". If we start off as a failure we will end up as a failure; if we begin life badly we are bound to finish life badly. Jesus Christ came to destroy this lie. He came to offer hope that we can change and can transform the failures and sinfulness which disfigure us so as to start living again with fresh hope.

With God there are no "hopeless cases". Even after living with Christ, hearing his words and witnessing his actions, the apostles let Jesus down by their betrayals and failure to understand him and the kind of healing love he offered. Yet Jesus reappeared to them after his resurrection to offer them peace. "Peace be with you", he said, "Receive the Holy Spirit". Jesus raised them up and encouraged them to start again.

And Jesus continues to encourage and to help us in the Sacrament of Reconciliation or confession. Many people still think of this sacrament as a "put down"— as the occasion when we try to remember our sins (almost every single one of them!) and receive a penance as a punishment for our past life. This is not at all how Christ himself saw and instituted this sacrament. For him it was an opportunity to give us new hope for the future and to lift us up to God's level.

When we celebrate the Sacrament of Reconciliation there are no set words to be learned although your child may be given some simple prayers as an initial introduction to the sacrament, but there are five key points to the sacrament. If you understand these points and can explain them to your child in ways which can be easily understood, your child will have a sound foundation in their understanding of this celebration of God's love for them.

Reflection

The starting point for reconciliation is not to think about our own life but to think about the words of Jesus. It is Jesus' life and words which give meaning to our own. So it's a good idea before receiving the sacrament to spend some time thinking about Christ, the kind of person he was, the things he did, and the way he treated people. It's helpful too, to remind ourselves of his death and resurrection and what those events mean for us today.

Examination

In the light of Christ's life we can then turn to our own life. It's not very helpful to try to remember everything – some people spend hours before they go to confession trying to recall every fault and failing. Or sometimes we spend ages trying to think of the best way of expressing our sins so that we don't appear worse than we really are. God isn't interested in how good a memory we have or how many failings we can discover in ourselves. He's interested only in restoring us, in being reconciled with us in love and healing, so he wants only our sorrow. When the prodigal son decided to return to his father, he prepared a little speech of apology. But before he could deliver it the Father was showering him with kisses of forgiveness and joy at his return. That's how it is with us and our heavenly Father in this sacrament.

...SSION?

Forgiveness

The priest after giving a penance, speaks Christ's words of forgiveness. People often question why we need to go to another human being to receive forgiveness and not go to God direct. The fact is that we are flesh and blood human beings and God communicates with us through human beings – beginning with Jesus Christ and then down the centuries through his ministers and our community of believers – the Church.
Through the priest God allows us to hear that our sins are forgiven.
Forgiveness brings us closer together then before.

Confession

When we go to the priest (either face to face or using a screen – the choice is up to us), we can let him be our guide. It's customary to let him know how long it is since our last confession and any particular things about the circumstances of our life which may be helpful for him to know. When we confess our sins there's no "right" or "wrong" way of doing so, it's entirely up to the individual, for what's important isn't what we say but what Christ says.

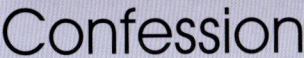

Sharing

God forgives us. But the sacrament is completed only when we return to our family and friends and share the forgiveness we have received. Too many of us are like the wicked steward in the Gospel who was forgiven a fortune by his Master and then bumped into a man who owed him only a few pence yet he insisted on repayment. The steward had failed totally to understand what had happened to him. It made no difference at all in his life. And it is the same with us. God's love and forgiveness makes all the difference to us. It makes it possible for us to start afresh in the confident knowledge that God loves us very much; and enables us to start again in offering his forgiveness to others.

RECONC

We convey our faith most clearly in the way we meet life. How do you react in times of stress and trouble? How do you respond to good times and happy experiences? Does your child "feel" the warmth of a living faith reflected in the lives of you and your partner? There may be some areas of life or relationships which you or your partner find difficult because of past experiences or your own upbringing. The following questions may help you to clarify some topics which have become difficult or perhaps even no-go areas for you. Talk about your reactions together or with a friend or your child's catechist. This will help you find the right ways forward for you to express your faith and your own feelings about reconciliation to your child.

Early Days
- What kind of relationship did you have with your mother?
- What kind of relationship did you have with your father?
- How were conflicts resolved in your family as a child? Did this reflect a Christian element of forgiveness and reconciliation?
- How able are you to say "sorry":
a) Very easily.
b) Only after some thought.
c) I find it very difficult, even impossible at times.
- How much do you think your answer to the above question is influenced by your childhood experiences of forgiveness and reconciliation.

Learning through sharing
- How easy is it for you to share yourself with other people?
- If you find it fairly easy can you say why?
- If you find it difficult can you say why?
- Think of a relationship which is important to you but which went wrong. Can you see the mistakes that were made by the other person? Can you see the mistakes you made?
- Are you close to anyone who has a very different vocation from you? If so, can you identify ways in which that helps you with your own vocation as a parent?
- Is there a relationship in your life which needs some attention? What can you do at this special time to begin to build a bridge?

Areas that stop us growing
- Were there some subjects that were taboo in your family life as a child? Can you list them?
- Why do you think these subjects were unmentionable? What made them no-go areas?
- How do you deal with those subjects in adult life today? Have you thought about them, tried to make sense of them, or not bothered too much about them? 
- What areas or topics do you find difficult to think about or deal with in your life now?
- Can you identify any reason for this?
- Choose one of your no-go areas, write it down and resolve to face it, think about it and begin to deal with it.

...ILIATION
THEN AND NOW

The part prayer plays in our life
- What prayer was there in your family life as a child?
- How has that influenced your prayer life today? Do you follow a similar pattern or pray in a very different way or not at all?
- When did you last try a new way of prayer or listen to another person's thoughts and experiences of prayer?
- When did you last mention your own prayer life to your partner, to anyone?
- How comfortable do you feel with your present prayer life? Is it a valuable part of your day, slightly boring, non-existent or a chore?
- What time will you set aside today to sit with God and tell him how you feel?

The prison of sin
- Can you identify what you consider to be the most serious area of sinfulness in yourself?
- When did this become a problem for you? Can you focus on the beginning?
- In what ways have you tried to deal with this problem; through confession, talking to a close friend, seeking others' advice? Have you put it from your mind or by other forms of self-discipline resigned yourself to living with it?
- Have you ever tried not trying anything but simply handing the problem to God and asking his help?
- Will you try risking the last suggestion?

The different kinds of prison
- What is your relationship with God? Are you angry with him? Are you afraid of God? Do you try to manipulate him?
- What is your relationship to those nearest to you? Do you find them difficult to deal with? Can you say why? What fault do they find in you?
- Do you despise certain groups of people? Can you say why?
- What do you most value in life in material terms? Are you too fond of this?
- What contribution do you make to the life of your Christian community?
- What kind of an example do you set your children/young people/your partner?

Identifying our needs and the possible healing needed
- When did you first learn about what was right and what was wrong?
- Looking back, was that introduction helpful or unhelpful? Jot down your reactions.
- What was the attitude of significant adults in your life towards accepting personal responsibility for their actions?
- What was their attitude towards forgiveness? Was it warm and generous or harsh and restrictive?
- How have these experiences affected your attitudes to your own weaknesses and responsibilities?
- Sin can often be a symptom of some more serious difficulty in our life. It can therefore be a mistake to try to deal with the sin instead of the underlying cause. Have you a recurring problem which you think may be a symptom of something deeper?

QUESTIONS AND ANSWERS

As a child, I was very frightened by going into the confessional box. How will my child receive the sacrament?

An important element of the Sacrament of Reconciliation is ensuring that there is genuine and comfortable communication between penitent and priest.
In most parishes now there is provision for the sacrament to be celebrated in a comfortable setting face to face. For those who prefer anonymity, a screen confessional is also provided. Your child is free to choose how he or she celebrates the sacrament.

My husband says he doesn't believe in God any more. How can I convince him?

You can't. You can only convince him that you believe in God. This is far more likely to help him than any direct attempt to change his mind.
Very few people indeed are non-believers for purely intellectual reasons. Nor will they be convinced by purely intellectual arguments. Most sincere non-believers reject God either because they see him as irrelevant to the world or because they can't reconcile God with the fact of so much suffering.
Your husband will be helped, then, by a faith which he sees to be relevant to your life as helping you to happiness; and a faith which he sees helps you to face your own sufferings with patience.
Sermons and generalities are certainly not going to win the day. People are more likely to be impressed when Christians openly and honestly share the doubts and struggles which have marked their own relationship with the Lord.

My divorce and remarriage prevents me from receiving the sacraments. How can I explain this to my daughter and encourage her to receive them?

First of all are you really sure that you cannot go to Holy Communion? Have you had your original marriage situation checked by a specialist in Marriage Tribunal work? Many Catholics, even today, believe that they cannot go to Holy Communion for various reasons simply because they have been told that they cannot by friends, relatives or even a priest or sister who have given a brief answer to their enquiry without knowing all the facts.

If, as you say, you are unable to receive Holy Communion then you must be honest with your daughter. Explain to her the love and teaching of Jesus Christ for all men and women and that this is the basis of the laws of the Church. Don't be afraid to tell her of your present situation, children can be very sympathetic and understanding when it comes to feeling uncomfortable or vulnerable. Explain that you have to wait before receiving Communion. Make your personal love of God very clear to her and this will demonstrate why it matters whether or not she receives the sacraments. The most important aspect of passing the faith on to your daughter is how you pray. If your prayer is natural and true your faith will make a lasting impression on your little girl. Your own private prayer and your prayers with her can be a real sharing in the life of the Church. Pope John Paul II encourages those who are in your situation to "listen to the word of God, to attend the sacrifice of the Mass, to persevere in prayer, to contribute to works of charity... to bring up your children in the Christian faith."

The faith my son is learning at his catechism class seems different from the one I learned as a child. This has made it much more difficult to answer his questions. For example, I was taught to go to Confession every month, his teacher refuses to put any time limits on going. Surely we need some rules?

The Church, like each one of us, is growing all the time for the Church is constantly moving towards fulfilment found in complete unity with God. This process of growth is as painful for the whole Church as it is for each one of us individually.

On the one hand, the Church is unchangeable in that she is built solidly on God's Word. On the other hand, she is constantly striving to give birth to that Word and to offer new life to each succeeding generation. Like Christ, the Church is divine and teaches the truth; but like Christ, she is also human and tries to adapt herself so as to bring as many people of goodwill as she can into her fold.

This is why the Church is constantly "changing". The passing of each generation brings a fresh appearance of the Church. Yet her essential personality remains the same. These changes in appearance can be confusing to many people. Yet without them the Church would stagnate.

The Sacrament of Reconciliation is one of the areas which the Church has adapted to today's world. Confession is meant to be a personal conversation between Christ and ourselves. Christ's words are more important than anything we have to say. This has led to less repetition of set formulae and less frequent confession. But the Church continues to remind us of its importance in helping us turn towards God.

What has happened to mortal sin? Everything seems so easy-going and too permissive these days.

As you will see from our history of this sacrament on pages 8-9 the ways in which we express our understanding of sin has developed and changed over the years. Until recently sin was often divided into mortal sin and venial sin. Mortal sin was a grievous offence against God which it was said "killed the soul". Venial sin was an offence which "displeased God and often lead to mortal sin". The purpose of this division was to distinguish between serious and less serious sin. As we can see from the teaching of Jesus in the Gospels, God never seeks the death or banishment of anyone. In fact the opposite; he constantly seeks out the lost, the abandoned and those who feel they are beyond hope or help. Clearly, he is not a God who wants to destroy his children. Rather, because of his great love for us, he gives us complete freedom to choose: freedom to choose whether we want to live as his children or whether we want to reject his teaching and his ways.

If we decide in that freedom, to reject him and to walk in other ways, we then segregate ourselves from him. We place ourselves outside his help and refuse his promises. In his great love for us he will not force us back. He only mourns our rejection of him.

If we decide in that freedom that we want to walk in his ways and try to follow his teaching, then God will never reject us or condemn us. When we fail, when we wander from his way, we will experience the alienation and pain felt when we put ourselves outside our heavenly Father's love. But as soon as we seek reconciliation it is ours, that is the promise of Christ. It is only when we refuse to accept his total offer of healing love and refuse to believe that reconciliation is offered by Christ that we cannot be forgiven and reconciled.

I'm not a Catholic and I feel unhappy about my daughter being subjected to this process of confession at such a young age. She is a good little girl and to start telling her she is a sinner seems destructive and damaging.

You are quite right in your instinct to want to prevent your daughter from being damaged by an unhappy or uncomfortable experience. The Sacrament of Reconciliation is in children's terms rather like "making-up" with God when we have turned away from his friendship. The concept of "making-up" is very familiar to all children as they negotiate friendships at school and at play. Most of us can remember the special rhymes and rituals from playground days associated with this developing understanding of the way we rebuild relationships which have become damaged or broken down.

Introducing children to the Sacrament of Reconciliation is part of the foundation of their personal relationship with God. They learn that however unfriendly they are towards God or other people, they can say "Sorry". They can be reconciled with their heavenly Father. At the heart of this teaching is the lesson that they are unconditionally loved. Throughout their life ahead God will never reject them, turn away from them or condemn them to isolation and despair. Such knowledge gives every person confidence to grow and reach their full potential as God intended them to.

PARENTS ARE THE KEY TO LOVE

"Can you tell me who made you?" the priest asked a small boy. The lad thought for a moment, then he looked up at the priest and said, "God made part of me."
"What do you mean, part of you?"
"Well," answered the boy, "God made me little,
I grew the rest myself."

"Growing the rest" is a lifetime job for all of us. God has fitted each of us to live one life – our own. We find personal wholeness and joy in discovering and using the particular gifts he has given us for living that life. "We are collaborators in creation" wrote Teilhard de Chardin. What each one of us is becoming is what the world is becoming. And each one of us makes a difference. You make a difference, your child makes a difference.

What do we imagine a "good Catholic parent" should be? Is it someone who can educate their children in the specific teachings and law of Christianity? Or is it someone who can nurture them in a way that their emotional and psychological growth can fully develop and mature? In a sense, the answer is "yes" to both questions but there can be a tendency to over-emphasise the first aspect, the teaching of the rules and system of our faith, at the expense of the nurturing side of faith development.

Throughout childhood we move through stages of development, thinking and morality. Our response to these stages is linked with our personal experiences, our relationship with our parents and family and our environment. The way in which your child negotiates or fails to negotiate these stages will lay the foundation for the development of faith in the future:

1. An ability to trust
Learning to trust or distrust is something we acquire in our earliest years. The experience of reliable, unconditional love forms the basis for learning, forgiveness, unselfishness and generous love.

2. Pre-conventional morality
Rules are kept simply to avoid punishment rather than for any concern about morality or the rightness of authority. Some actions satisfy certain needs, for example the need to be accepted or rewarded.

3. Conventional morality
A child begins to develop loyalty to the group, family or school. As relationships develop and new relationships are formed, right behaviour in order to seek the approval and acceptance by these groups is seen as important.

4. Pre-adolescence
Personal religious thought begins to develop and we begin to learn to be ourselves and make more personal decisions with less reference to the approval or otherwise of the group or family.

From this basic outline it is clear that there are certain limits to what we can teach a young child in any formal sense. What is confirmed is that the old saying, "Faith is caught not taught" is significant.

Faith is not simply knowing about God, it is knowing God in a personal way, and in life we learn about personal love in and through other people from the moment of our birth, long before we having any teaching in a formal sense. Children are born with feelings and to dismiss the emotional elements of faith learning is a serious mistake.

Key points in passing on the faith in a practical and realistic way which your child can build upon in the years ahead:

It's important that your child learns to give and receive affection, develop confidence and is able to seek reassurance.

Try to share with your child what is meaningful to them in your love relationship with God.

Sharing thanksgiving (grace at mealtimes), preparation and celebration of key seasons (Advent, Lent), prayer as a simple form of showing confidence and trust in God who is all-loving, faithful and trustworthy; these are always of laying a sound foundation for faith development.

Text: Rosemary Gallagher
Design: JELLY DESIGN
Photographs:
Image Bank, Photonica and APA
First Printed   May 1993
Redesigned   June 1999
Copyright © Redemptorist Publications

All rights reserved. No part of this publication may be reproduced, stored in a retrieval system, or transmitted in any form or by any means, electronic, mechanical, photocopying, recording or otherwise, without prior permission in writing from Redemptorist Publications.
ISBN 0 85231 139 7
A Registered Charity limited by guarantee. Registered in England 3261721.

Nihil Obstat: Cyril Murtagh, V.G.
Censor Deputatus
Imprimatur + Crispian Hollis
Episcopus Portus Magni
Portus Magni April 1993
The Nihil Obstat and Imprimatur are a declaration that a book or pamphlet is considered to be free from doctrinal or moral error. It is not implied that those who have granted the Nihil Obstat and Imprimatur agree with the contents, opinions and statements expressed

Redemptorist
PUBLICATIONS
Alphonsus House Chawton Hampshire GU34 3HQ
Telephone 01420 88222   Fax 01420 88805
rp@redempt.org   www.redempt.org

Printed by: Knight & Willson Limited Leeds LS11 5SF